BIRDS
CROSS STITCH

Project Book

Learn how to cross stitch with
these beautiful bird designs

10 patterns inside

INTRODUCTION

Cross stitch is a relaxing craft that is easy to learn.

With an almost unlimited range of designs, cross stitch can be customised in so many ways.

We have included everything you need to help start your cross stitch journey and stitch your very own blue tit. Once you've learnt the basics, you can try the other nature inspired patterns provided, including a flamingo, robin, puffin and many more.

This book will introduce you to cross stitch and give you a range of beautiful bird designs to get you started.

WHAT IS INCLUDED IN YOUR KIT:

14ct cotton aida
Metal needle
5 x Embroidery thread skeins
6" Plastic embroidery hoop

WHAT YOU'LL NEED:

Sharp scissors

3

TIPS & TECHNIQUES

TIP 1: Trailing threads

Avoid trailing your thread between areas of colour where there are no stitches. Sometimes these can show through your aida and affect your design. Make sure you finish one section, tie off your thread and move to the next one.

TIP 2: Where to start?

Always start by stitching the largest colour area first, followed by the smaller blocks of colour.

TIP 3: Stitching rows

If you are stitching a long row of crosses in the same colour, stitch a row of half crosses and then go back and complete the crosses as a row.

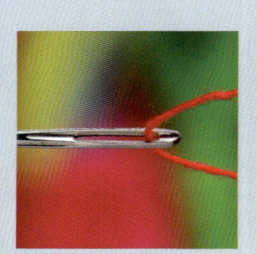

TIP 4: Cross Consistency

To keep your stitches looking consistent, always stitch the first half of the cross in the same direction. For example, always start with the stitch from top left to bottom right.

MATERIALS

AIDA

Aida is a stiff fabric with clearly defined holes that makes stitching on it super easy for beginners. It is available in a range of colours and counts.
The aida count refers to the number of stitches per inch, 14 count is the most popular for beginners as you can clearly see the holes to stitch in.
Once you're comfortable you can move to an aida with more stitches per inch, this will offer a more intricate design.
Make sure to use a substantial sized aida so you have plenty to work with when mounting or framing later.

NEEDLE

Most sizes or types of needle will work fine for cross stitch so you want to try out a few and see what feels best for you and the fabric you choose.
A tapestry needle with a large eye and blunt tip will work well as it makes threading easier and will stitch easily without piercing or splitting the threads.

THREAD

When cross stitching you will need to use stranded thread —cotton or polyester will work well. This can be separated into six individual strands, allowing you to use how ever many are needed at a time for your particular project or stitch type. Most cross stitch uses two strands of thread whilst backstitch uses just one. To separate the strands, cut a 50cm length and pull one of the loose ends gently. Do this slowly with each strand to prevent any tangling or knots. You can now use the required number of strands as stated in your pattern.
All of the projects included in this book are based on DMC thread colours.

CHART

Each cross stitch design will be shown as a gridded chart which clearly shows where to stitch each colour. The chart is accompanied by a key with symbols that represent your thread colour, making it easy to follow.

THE HOOP FRAME

Although using a hoop isn't essential, it can help to hold your work in place whilst you stitch, keeping the fabric taut and your stitches even. You can choose from a range of sizes and materials so experiment and see what you find most comfortable. Hoops are also great for displaying your finished piece - so consider a material and colour that suits your interior.

SETTING UP YOUR HOOP:

Loosen the screw on the embroidery hoop (without removing) and separate the two parts of the hoop.

Place the aida fabric centrally over the inner hoop.

Place the outer hoop on top of the aida and press down firmly so both hoops are level, trapping the fabric in-between.
Tighten the screw to secure the fabric, making sure it's taut.
If your design is larger than the hoop, simply unscrew the hoop and move the fabric so the next section is central.

FINDING YOUR CENTRE:

To ensure your design is centred on the fabric, start in the middle of your project and work your way out. To find the centre, fold your fabric in half vertically, then horizontally. Where those folds meet is the centre point.

Now find the centre of your cross stitch pattern. Sometimes this is clearly marked with arrows on either side of the grid. If not, fold your pattern the same way you did your fabric and mark the centre stitch. This will be your first stitch

TIP
Don't leave your fabric in the hoop for a long period of time whilst you're not stitching, as the tension will stretch the fabric and the creases will be harder to remove.

7

TYPES OF STITCHING

WHOLE STITCHES

Bring the needle up in the bottom left corner of a square on the fabric and down again in the top right corner, making the first half of the cross.
Next, bring the needle up through the fabric at the top corner and down again through the bottom right. This completes the first cross stitch. (pic a)
If you're completing a row of stitches, sew a row of your first diagonal stitch and then come back with the top diagonal stitch to complete all crosses. (pic b)

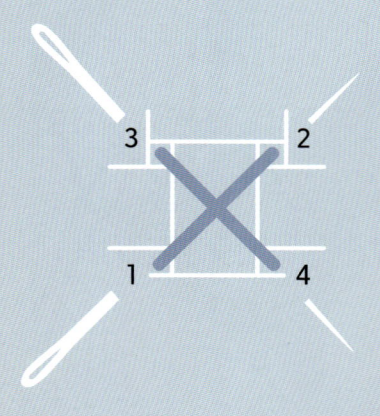

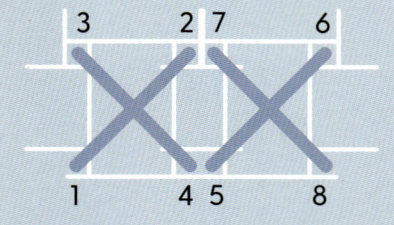

FRACTIONAL STITCHES

Some designs will include fractional stitches to give the edge of your design a smoother look.

¾ Stitch – These are indicated on the chart and are similar to whole stitches. The only difference is that one half of the stitch will pierce the strands of aida in the centre of where the stitch will sit, with the second half being added in the opposite direction to complete the stitch.

¼ Stitch – These are made of a single stitch, thread your needle through a few of the vertical stitches on the reverse of your work to secure before cutting the excess thread. Do not tie as a knot as this will create lumps in your work.

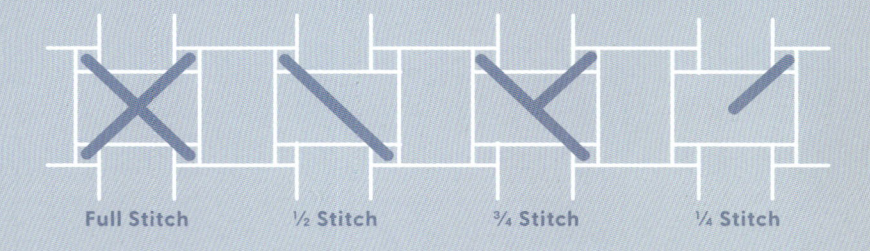

Full Stitch **½ Stitch** **¾ Stitch** **¼ Stitch**

BACK STITCH

The Backstitch is used to outline your work and give definition to a cross stitch design. It is usually stitched with one strand of cotton and can be made horizontally, vertically or diagonally across single or multiple squares. To start, weave your needle through the back of several stitches to secure the end of the thread. Bring the needle up through the fabric and down one hole back, up again, then down. This should be added to your work once all cross stitches have been completed.

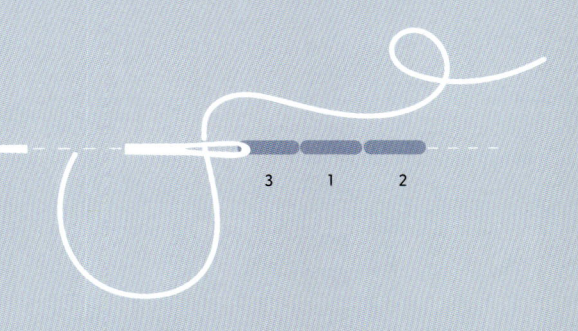

3 1 2

MAKES 1

2 HRS TO MAKE

BLUE TIT

BLUE TIT

YOU WILL NEED
- Sharp scissors

KIT CONTENTS
- 14ct cotton aida
- Metal needle
- 5 x Embroidery thread
- 6" Plastic embroidery hoop

METHOD

With splashes of blue and yellow, this eye-catching bird is one of the most recognisable garden visitors. Sure to be loved by any green-fingered friend.

Fabric: 14 Count Aida
Stitches: 72 x 54
Size: 5.14 x 3.86 inches or 13.06 x 9.80 cm
Colours: DMC

Use 2 strands of thread to cross stitch

KEY

Colour Ref		Cross Stitch
535	Stone Grey	■ ☐
522	Trellis Green	■ ▽
834	Light Brass	■ ●
B5200	Bright White	☐ ●
931	Blue Grey	■ ◨

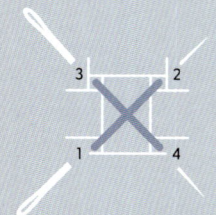

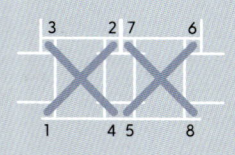

WHOLE STITCH:

13

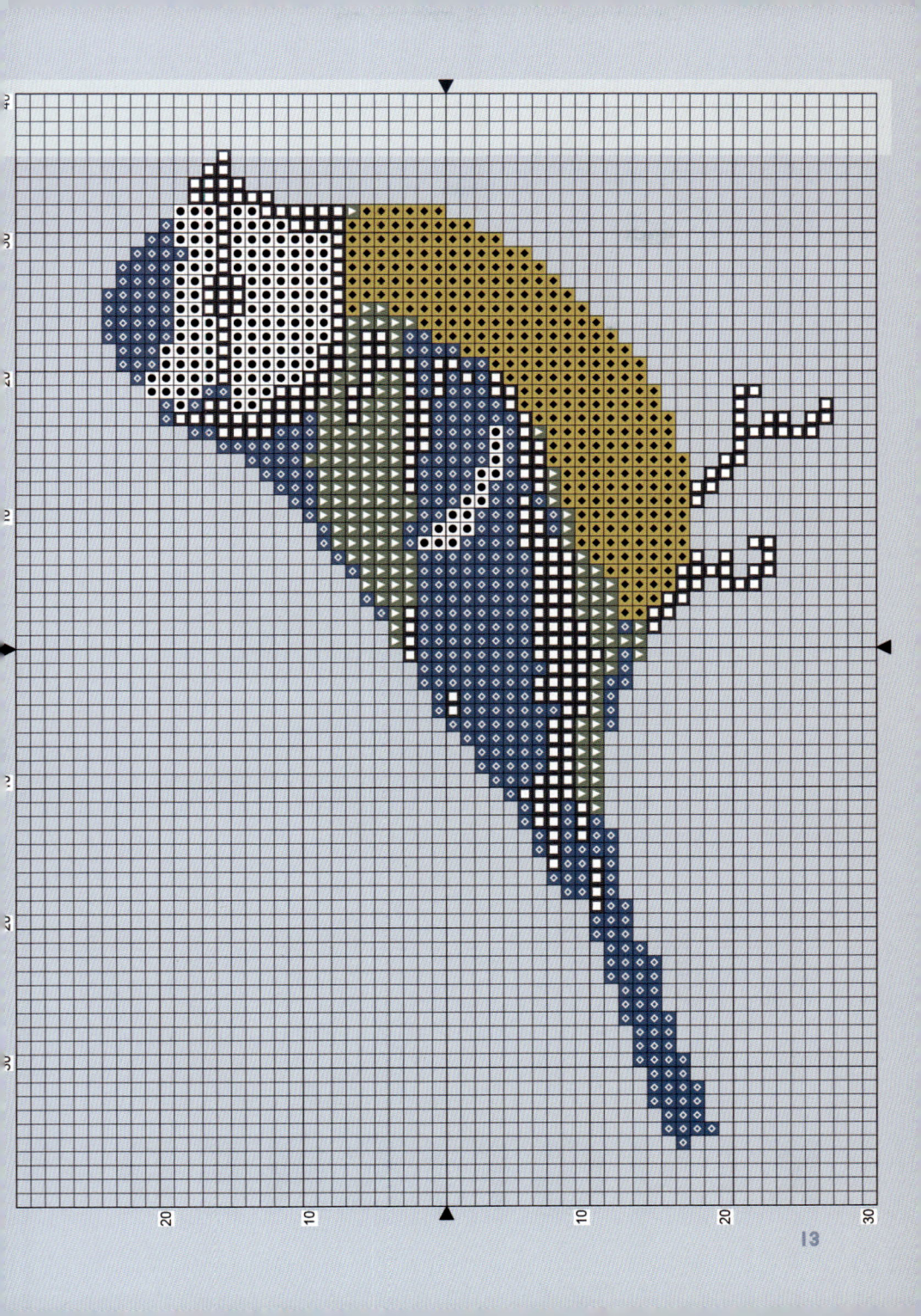

MAKES 1

2 HRS TO MAKE

KINGFISHER

KINGFISHER

YOU WILL NEED
- Sharp scissors
- 6" Plastic embroidery hoop
- Metal needle

MATERIALS
- 14ct cotton aida
- Embroidery thread

15

METHOD

This colourful and unmistakeable bird is usually found in tropical surroundings. Stitch and display in your home for a touch of paradise.

Fabric: 14 Count Aida
Stitches: 65 x 68
Size: 4.64 x 4.86 inches or 11.79 x 12.34 cm
Colours: DMC

Use 2 strands of thread to cross stitch

KEY

Colour Ref		Cross Stitch	
807	Pond Blue	▪	●
977	Caramel Brown	▪	O
B5200	Bright White Cream	▫	⌐
3866	Garlic Cream	▫	+
163	Eucalyptus	▪	◣
725	Sunlight Yellow	▪	▼
535	Stone Grey	▪	▪

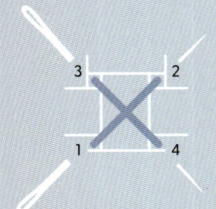

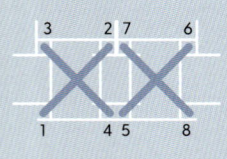

WHOLE STITCH:

16

17

MAKES 1 **2 HRS TO MAKE**

PUFFIN

PUFFIN

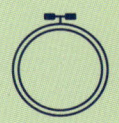

YOU WILL NEED
- 6" Plastic embroidery hoop
- Sharp scissors
- Metal needle

MATERIALS
- 14ct cotton aida
- Embroidery thread

19

METHOD

Known for being the clown amongst sea birds, the puffin is the perfect uplifting character for a pick me up.

Fabric: 14 Count Aida
Stitches: 64 x 58
Size: 4.57 x 4.14 inches or 11.61 x 10.52 cm
Colours: DMC

Use 2 strands of thread to cross stitch

KEY

Colour Ref		Cross Stitch	
3799	Anthracite Grey	■	■
318	Granite Grey	■	▼
762	Pearl Grey	■	◣
939	Dark Navy Blue	■	■
3078	Pale Yellow	■	□
4	Dark Tin	■	●
722	Orange Spice	■	◇
413	Iron Grey	■	■
3865	Winter White	■	◣

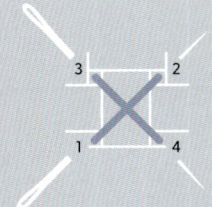

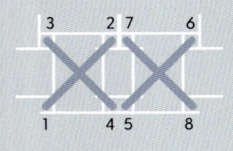

WHOLE STITCH:

20

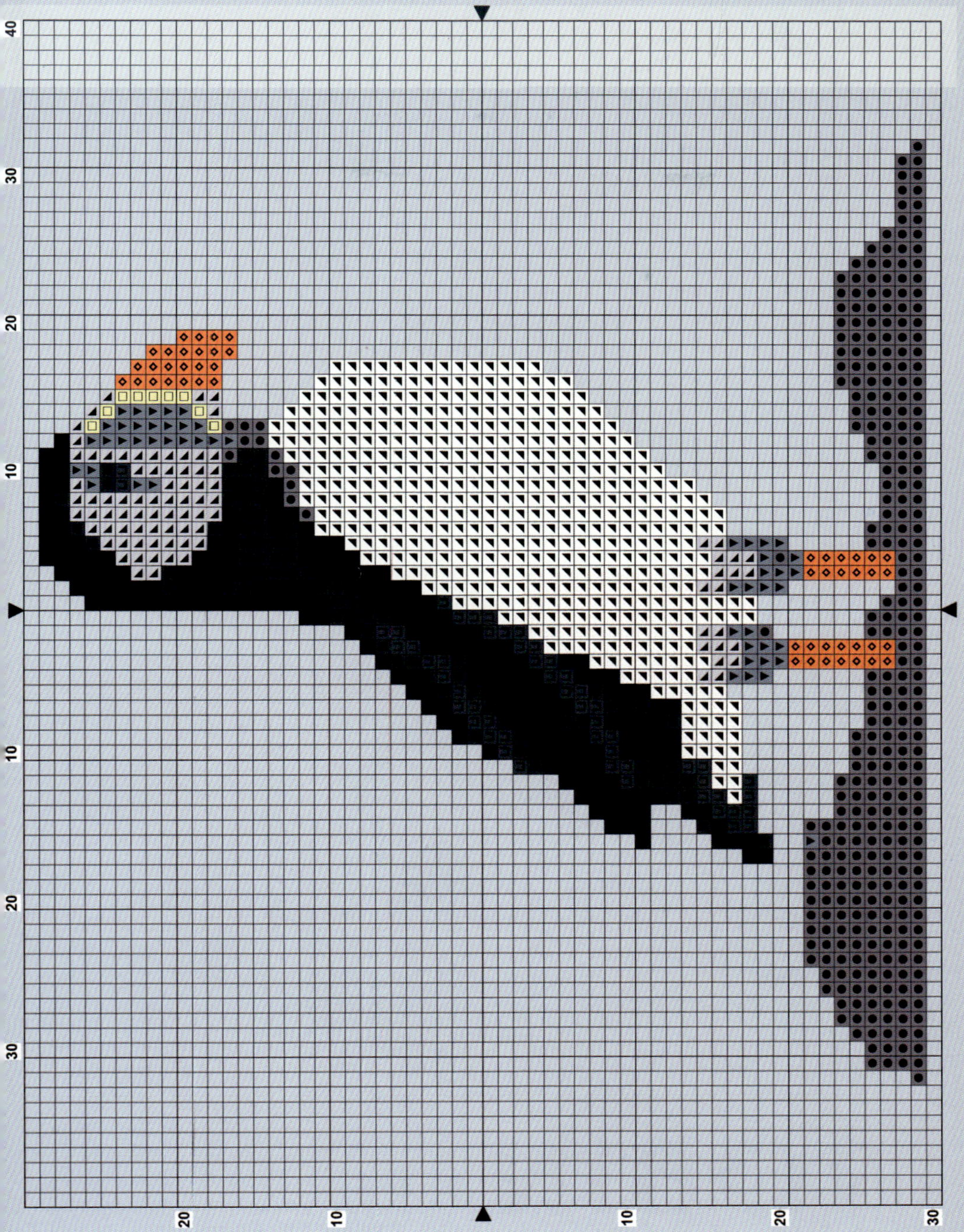

MAKES 1

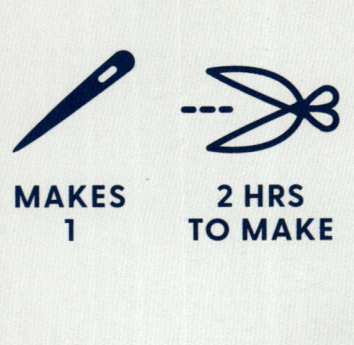

2 HRS TO MAKE

ROBIN

ROBIN

YOU WILL NEED
- 6" Plastic embroidery hoop
- Sharp scissors
- Metal needle

MATERIALS
- 14ct cotton aida
- Embroidery thread

METHOD

The nations favourite! This bird can be seen all year round but is known to be a feature during the festive season. Add this red-breasted beauty to your Christmas décor.

Fabric: 14 Count Aida
Stitches: 58 x 48
Size: 4.14 x 3.43 inches or 10.52 x 8.71 cm
Colours: DMC

Use 2 strands of thread to cross stitch

KEY

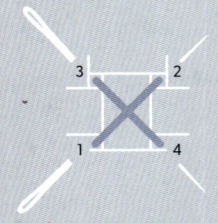

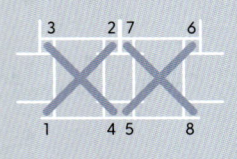

Colour Ref		Cross Stitch
640	Green Grey	■ ■
720	Rust	■ ◆
B5200	Bright White	□ ◢
647	Rock Grey	■ ●
370	Medium Mustard	■ ◣
844	Black Pepper	■ ■

WHOLE STITCH:

48

METHOD

* **You will need & materials are the same as the other bird makes.**

With their distinctive hair-dos, cockatiels are quirky characters! They depend upon companionship for a long and happy life – making this perfect to stitch for someone you cherish.

Fabric: 14 Count Aida
Stitches: 47 x 74
Size: 3.36 x 5.29 inches or 8.53 x 13.43 cm
Colours: DMC

Use 2 strands of thread to cross stitch

KEY

Colour Ref		Cross Stitch	Colour Ref		Cross Stitch
647	Rock Grey		973	Daffodil Yellow	
1	White Tin		844	Pepper Black	
744	Grapefruit Yellow		648	Pepper Grey	
5	Light Driftwood		746	Vanilla	
3866	Garlic Cream		3854	Spicey Gold	

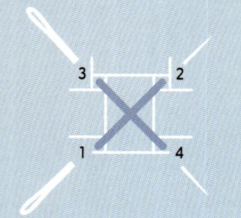

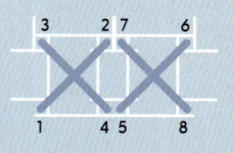

WHOLE STITCH:

47

MAKES 1
2 HRS TO MAKE

COCKATIEL

45

METHOD

This striking Native American bird symbolises trust and loyalty – gift it to a loved one to show them you care.

Fabric: 14 Count Aida
Stitches: 62 x 72
Size: 4.43 x 5.14 inches or 11.25 x 13.06 cm
Colours: DMC

Use 2 strands of thread to cross stitch

KEY

Colour Ref		Cross Stitch	Colour Ref		Cross Stitch
535	Stone Grey		762	Pearl Grey	×
3865	Winter White	▽	930	Slate Grey	◆
414	Lead Grey	◆	312	Night Blue	◣
3839	Mediterranean Blue	◣	322	Delft Blue	◣
4	Dark Tin	◆	799	Horizon Blue	U
809	Gentle Blue	O	932	Seagull Blue	□
157	Light Cornflower Blue	▽	415	Chrome Grey	+
			1	White Tin	◿

WHOLE STITCH:

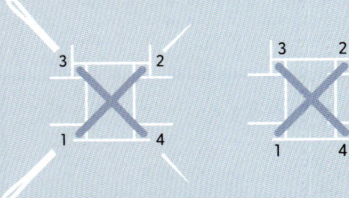

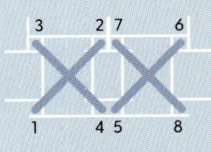

BLUE JAY

YOU WILL NEED

- 6" Plastic embroidery hoop
- Sharp scissors
- Metal needle

MATERIALS

- 14ct cotton aida
- Embroidery thread

43

MAKES 1

2 HRS TO MAKE

BLUE JAY

41

METHOD

As the nations only naturalised parrot, these green birds bring a touch of the tropics to their urban habitats.

Fabric: 14 Count Aida
Stitches: 51 x 69
Size: 3.64 x 4.93 inches or 9.25 x 12.52 cm
Colours: DMC

Use 2 strands of thread to cross stitch

KEY

Colour Ref		Cross Stitch	Colour Ref		Cross Stitch
535	Stone Grey		986	Dark Forest Green	
3346	Hunter Green		3810	Dark Turquoise	
989	Fennel Green		223	Medium Dusty Pink	
3348	Lettuce Heart Green		Blanc	Blanc	
2	Tin		17	Light Yellow Plum	

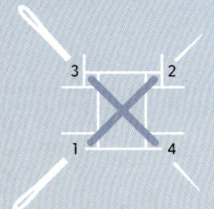

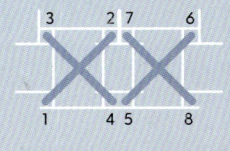

WHOLE STITCH:

PARAKEET

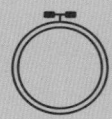

YOU WILL NEED

- 6" Plastic embroidery hoop
- Sharp scissors
- Metal needle

MATERIALS

- 14ct cotton aida
- Embroidery thread

MAKES
1

2 HRS
TO MAKE

PARAKEET

38

37

METHOD

In rainbow colours, this vibrant and chatty parrot is sure to bring colour and joy. Stitch one for a friend in need of some sunshine!

Fabric: 14 Count Aida
Stitches: 51 x 66
Size: 3.64 x 4.71 inches or 9.25 x 11.97 cm
Colours: DMC

Use 2 strands of thread to cross stitch

KEY

Colour Ref		Cross Stitch	Colour Ref		Cross Stitch
3371	Ebony		803	Ink Blue	
825	Sea Blue		3863	Otter Brown	
813	Light Blue		900	Saffron Orange	
721	Papaya Orange		3820	Maze Yellow	
712	Cream		632	Cocoa	

WHOLE STITCH:

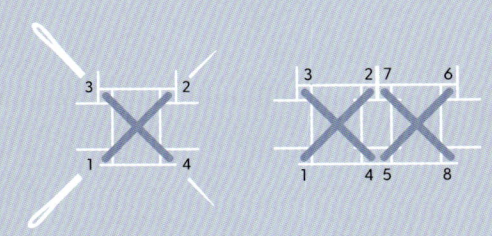

PARROT

YOU WILL NEED
- 6" Plastic embroidery hoop
- Sharp scissors
- Metal needle

MATERIALS
- 14ct cotton aida
- Embroidery thread

35

MAKES 1

2 HRS TO MAKE

PARROT

33

METHOD

The wise owl is known for being nocturnal and comes alive at night – why not stitch and gift to the night owl in your life.

Fabric: 14 Count Aida
Stitches: 57 x 69
Size: 4.07 x 4.93 inches or 10.34 x 12.52 cm
Colours: DMC

Use 2 strands of thread to cross stitch

KEY

Colour Ref		Cross Stitch	Colour Ref		Cross Stitch
3371	Ebony		3033	Antique Silver	
3790	Cappaucino Brown		3021	Cliff Grey	
640	Green Grey		8	Dark Driftwood	
642	Earth Grey		647	Rock Grey	
3023	Light Platinum Grey		612	String Brown	
842	Beige Rope		3782	Gingerbread Brown	
644	Light Green Grey		3046	Rye Beige	
			5	Light Driftwood	

WHOLE STITCH:

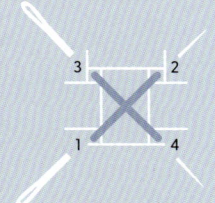

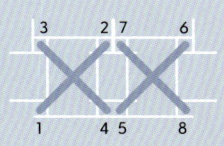

OWL

YOU WILL NEED

- 6" Plastic embroidery hoop
- Sharp scissors
- Metal needle

MATERIALS

- 14ct cotton aida
- Embroidery thread

MAKES 1

2 HRS TO MAKE

OWL

30

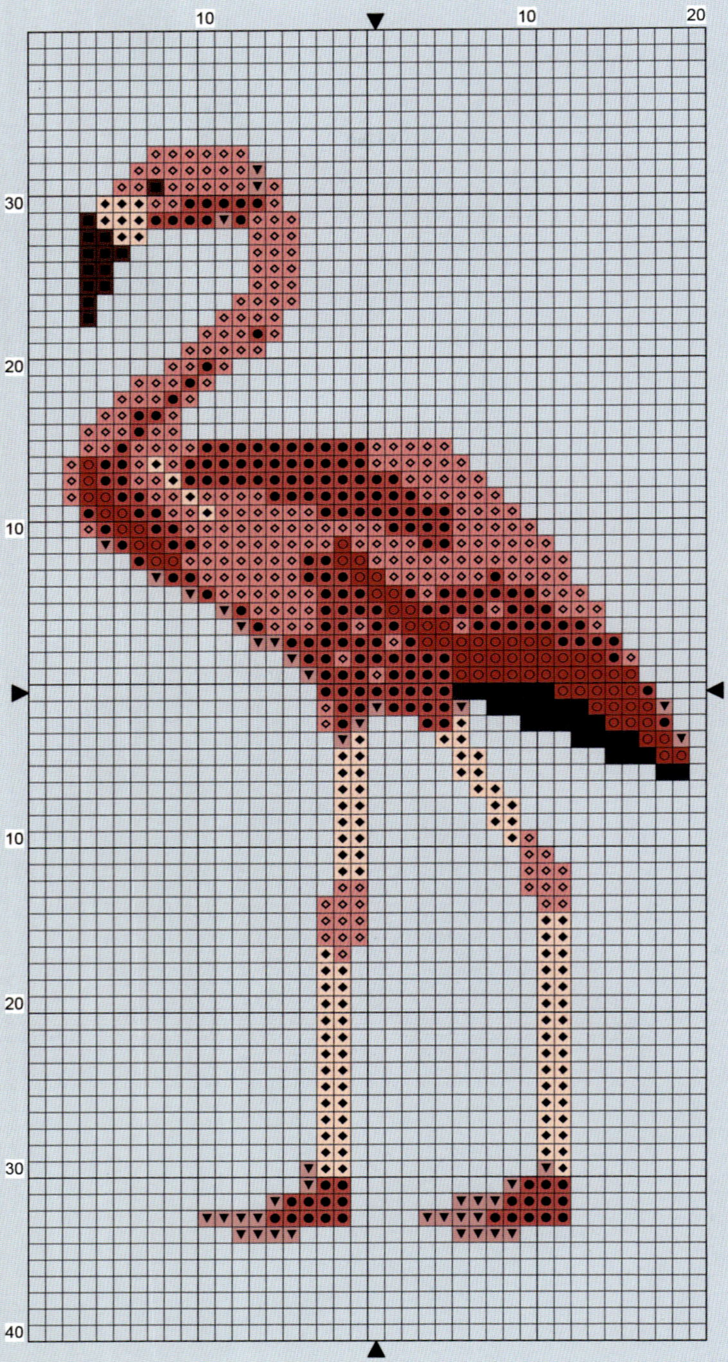

10
10
20
30
20
10
10
20
30
40

METHOD

Pretty in Pink! These beautiful birds are known to form long-lasting and loyal friendships – show your love and affection, and stitch for a loved one.

Fabric: 14 Count Aida
Stitches: 37 x 67
Size: 2.64 x 4.79 inches or 6.71 x 12.16 cm
Colours: DMC

Use 2 strands of thread to cross stitch

KEY

Colour Ref		Cross Stitch
3857	Dark Red Wine	■ ■
152	Antique Rose	▮ ▼
967	Pale Apricot	▮ ◆
817	Japenese Red	■ ●
3328	Dark Salmon	■ ●
760	Grenadine Pink	▮ ◇
939	Dark Navy Blue	■ ■

WHOLE STITCH:

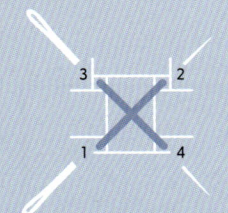

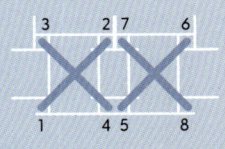

28

FLAMINGO

YOU WILL NEED
- 6" Plastic embroidery hoop
- Sharp scissors
- Metal needle

MATERIALS
- 14ct cotton aida
- Embroidery thread

MAKES 1

2 HRS TO MAKE

FLAMINGO

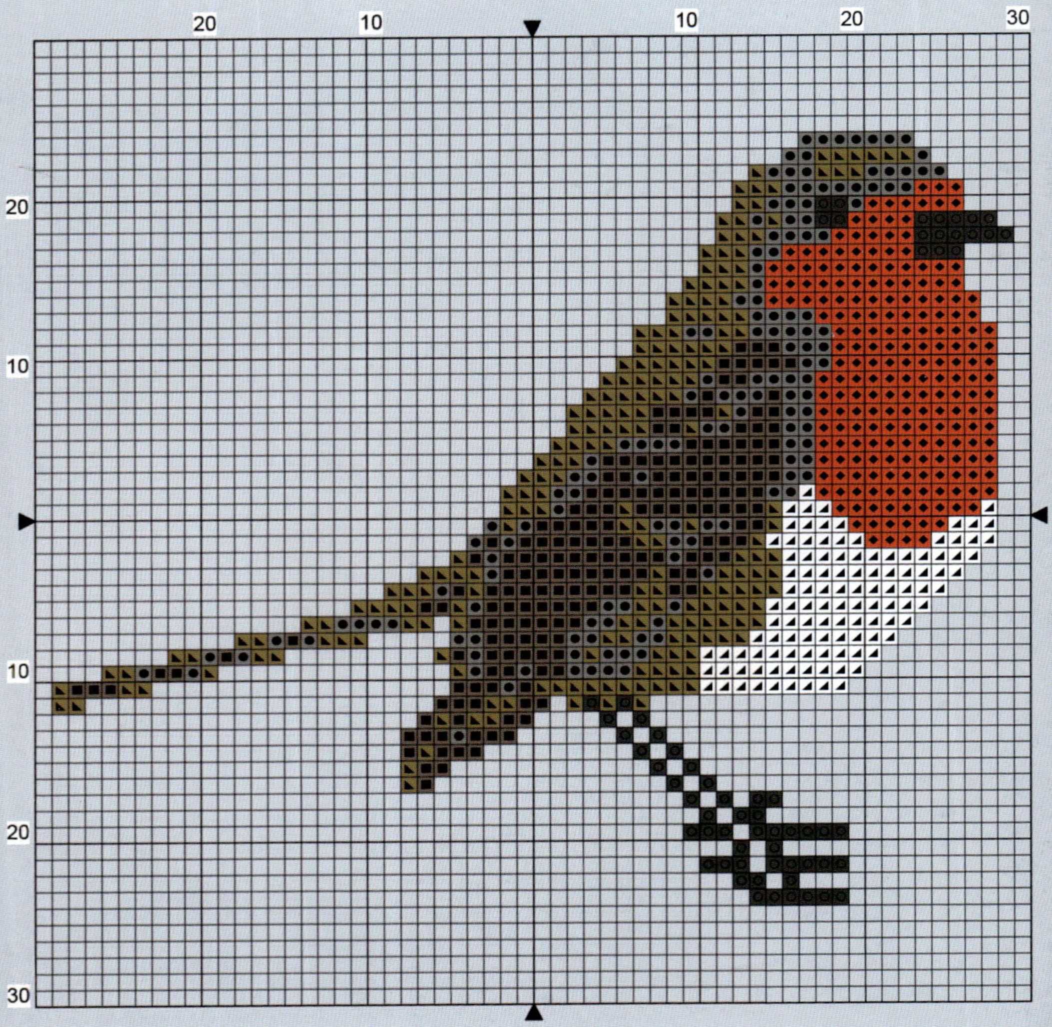
20
10
10
20
30
20
10
10
20
30